GA

CENGAGE Learning

Novels for Students, Volume 14

Staff

Editor: Jennifer Smith.

Contributing Editors: Anne Marie Hacht, Michael L. LaBlanc, Ira Mark Milne, Daniel Toronto, Carol Ullmann.

Managing Editor, Content: Dwayne D. Hayes.

Managing Editor, Product: David Galens.

Publisher, Literature Product: Mark Scott.

Literature Content Capture: Joyce Nakamura, *Managing Editor*. Sara Constantakis, *Editor*.

Research: Victoria B. Cariappa, *Research Manager*. Sarah Genik, Ron Morelli, Tamara Nott, Tracie A. Richardson, *Research Associates*. Nicodemus Ford, *Research Assistant*.

Permissions: Maria L. Franklin, *Permissions Manager*. Shalice Shah-Caldwell, *Permissions*

Associate. Deborah Freitas, *IC Coordinator/Permissions Associate.*

Manufacturing: Mary Beth Trimper, *Manager, Composition and Electronic Prepress.* Evi Seoud, *Assistant Manager, Composition Purchasing and Electronic Prepress.* Stacy Melson, *Buyer.*

Imaging and Multimedia Content Team: Barbara Yarrow, *Manager.* Randy Bassett, *Imaging Supervisor.* Robert Duncan, Dan Newell, Luke Rademacher, *Imaging Specialists.* Pamela A. Reed, *Imaging Coordinator.* Leitha Etheridge-Sims, Mary Grimes, David G. Oblender, *Image Catalogers.* Robyn V. Young, *Project Manager.* Dean Dauphinais, *Senior Image Editor.* Kelly A. Quin, *Image Editor.*

Product Design Team: Pamela A. E. Galbreath, *Senior Art Director.* Michael Logusz, *Graphic Artist.*

Copyright Notice

agency, institution, publication, service, or individual does not imply endorsement of the editors or publisher. Errors brought to the attention of the publisher and verified to the satisfaction of the publisher will be corrected in future editions.

ISBN 0-7876-4897-3
ISSN 1094-3552

Printed in the United States of America.

10 9 8 7 6 5 4 3 2 1

Oliver Twist

Charles Dickens

1838

Introduction

Oliver Twist, published in 1838, is one of Charles Dickens's best-known and well-loved works. It was written after he had already attained success as the author of *The Pickwick Papers*. It has been adapted as a film and a long-running Broadway musical and has been considered a classic ever since it was first published. The book originally appeared as a "serial"; that is, each chapter was published separately, in order, in a magazine called *Bentley's Miscellany*, of which Dickens was editor. Each week, readers waited avidly for the next installment in the tale; this partly accounts for the fact that each chapter ends with a "cliff-hanger" that would hold the reader's interest until the following chapter was published.

Dickens uses the characters and situations in the book to make a pointed social commentary, attacking the hypocrisy and flaws of institutions, including his society's government, its laws and criminal system, and its methods of dealing with poor people. Interestingly, he doesn't suggest any solutions; he merely points out the suffering inflicted by these systems and their deep injustice. Dickens basically believed that most people were good at heart but that their good impulses could be distorted by social ills.

After publishing *Oliver Twist*, Dickens went on to write *Nicholas Nickelby, The Old Curiosity Shop, Barnaby Rudge, American Notes, Martin Chuzzlewit, Dombey and Son, David Copperfield, Bleak House, Hard Times, Little Dorrit, A Tale of Two Cities, Great Expectations, Our Mutual Friend*, and *The Mystery of Edwin Drood*. After 1858 he often toured, reading out loud from his works to huge audiences; every new piece from his pen was eagerly awaited, and he was perhaps the most famous and best-loved author who has ever lived.

Author Biography

Charles Dickens was born on February 7, 1812, in Portsea, England. His father, John Dickens, was a navy clerk. In 1814, John Dickens was transferred to London, and in 1817, the whole family moved to Chatham, near the naval docks. Dickens's life during the next five years was stable and happy; he was tutored by his mother and later went to school in Chatham. His father had a small collection of books, and Dickens read them avidly.

In 1822, Dickens's father was transferred back to London, but he had gotten himself deeply in debt by then and was soon sent to a debtors' prison, or workhouse, along with his wife and Dickens's siblings. Dickens, who at twelve was considered old enough to work, had to work in a boot-blacking warehouse. Alone in a strange city, separated from his family, he endured harrowing experiences that marked him with a hatred for the social system and the desire to succeed so that he would never have to live this way again. After a few months, he was saved when his grandmother died and her small legacy allowed Dickens's father to get out of prison.

When he was fifteen, Dickens became a clerk in a solicitor's office, and at sixteen, he became a court reporter, a job that taught him much about London and all its people. In 1932, he became a journalist, and in 1834, he became a staff writer for the well-known *Morning Chronicle*. He was soon known as one of the best reporters in the city. He used these experiences to write anonymous pieces, titled "Sketches by Boz," for the *Monthly Magazine*. Gradually, however, his anonymity faded, and the name "Dickens" began attracting attention. In 1836, *Sketches by Boz, Illustrative of Everyday Life* was published, followed by a second series, and the complete sketches were published in 1839.

Also in 1836, the first number of *The Posthumous Papers of the Pickwick Club* was published. Eventually, printing of the stories rose from 400 to 40,000, a number that would be large for a new author even today.

Flushed with his success, Dickens married Catherine Hogarth, the daughter of a newspaper editor, in April of 1836. They had ten children and remained married for twenty-two years but eventually would become incompatible and separate.

After publishing *Oliver Twist* (1838), Dickens went on to write *Nicholas Nickelby* (1838–1839), *The Old Curiosity Shop* (1840–1841), *Barnaby Rudge* (1841), *American Notes* (1842), *Martin Chuzzlewit* (1843–1844), *Dombey and Son* (1846–1848), *David Copperfield* (1849–1850), *Bleak House* (1852–1853), *Hard Times* (1854), *Little Dorrit* (1855–1857), *A Tale of Two Cities* (1859), *Great Expectations* (1860–1861), *Our Mutual Friend* (1864–1865), and *The Mystery of Edwin Drood* (1870, unfinished).

Dickens also wrote short stories, travel pieces,

and dramas. He was the editor of *Household Words* and *All the Year Round*, well-known periodicals of his day.

After 1858, he often toured, reading out loud from his works to huge audiences; every new piece from his pen was eagerly awaited, and he was perhaps the most famous and best-loved author who has ever lived. He died on June 8, 1870, while working on his last book, *The Mystery of Edwin Drood*. He is buried in Westminster Abbey, one of the highest honors in England.

Plot Summary

Chapters One through Nine

The book opens with Oliver's birth in a workhouse, as his unmarried and nameless mother dies. He is soon transferred to an "infant farm," run by Mrs. Mann, who starves the children under her care and pockets the money given to her for their food. Although many of the children die, investigations always determine that the death was "accidental." Oliver lives with her until he is nine, when the parish beadle, Mr. Bumble, arrives to tell her that Oliver is supposed to return to the workhouse. At the workhouse, he gets in trouble for asking for more food. For this audacious behavior, he is locked up, and the workhouse board decides to give five pounds to anyone who will take Oliver as an apprentice and thus relieve the parish of his care.

A chimney sweep, Gamfield, offers to take Oliver but is rejected when a kindly magistrate finds that Oliver is terrified of Gamfield. He goes back to the workhouse until an undertaker, Mr. Sowerberry, agrees to take him. At Sowerberry's house he must sleep among the half-built coffins and eat leftovers even the dog won't touch. In addition, he is bullied by Noah Claypole, another charity boy who works for Sowerberry, and by Charlotte, Sowerberry's servant.

Sowerberry decides to have Oliver work as a

hired mourner at children's funerals, because he looks so unhappy all the time. This promotion makes Claypole furiously jealous, and he attacks Oliver, who violently defends himself, hitting the much bigger Claypole to the floor. Sowerberry beats Oliver and then locks him up until bedtime.

The next morning, Oliver runs away to London. On his way out of town, he stops to say goodbye to Dick, a younger, frailer child who was his best friend at Mrs. Mann's.

On the road to London, Oliver is starving and exhausted. He begs for food and sleeps outside. He meets a strange boy, dressed in a large man's coat, who seems very street-smart. This boy, Jack Dawkins, otherwise known as the Artful Dodger, offers to introduce Oliver to a man who will give him free housing.

In London, they make their way to a dirty, dangerous street and enter a run-down house, where a filthy old man greets them. This is Fagin, the leader of a group of child criminals. Oliver falls asleep but wakes to see Fagin gloating over a treasure. Fagin explains that this is his life savings, but, in fact, it's stolen goods. Later, the Dodger comes in with another boy, Charley Bates, and they practice picking Fagin's pockets.

Chapters Ten through Nineteen

Oliver sometimes takes part in this game, but he doesn't realize yet that it is practice for stealing. He thinks Fagin is respectable and is simply teaching the boys good work ethics. He begs to be allowed to go out with Charley and the Dodger and gets into trouble when they pick a man's pocket and then run away. Oliver doesn't run, and he's immediately grabbed as the thief. He is shocked, having finally realized that his "friends" are all thieves.

He is taken to the police station, and the man who accused him, Mr. Brownlow, follows. This man has second thoughts about the accusation because Oliver doesn't look like a thief. Oliver also looks familiar to him, although he doesn't know why. In the courtroom, an evil magistrate, Mr. Fang, sentences him to three months of hard labor. Oliver faints. Another witness shoves into the courtroom and reports that he saw the whole crime and that Oliver is innocent. Oliver is released, but he is weak and disoriented. Mr. Brownlow takes Oliver home with him.

Oliver remains unconscious for several days. Mrs. Bedwin, Brownlow's housekeeper, takes care of him. At Brownlow's house, he is fascinated by a portrait of a kind-looking woman on the wall. Brownlow notices that Oliver resembles the woman.

Meanwhile, Dawkins and the Dodger have gone back to Fagin's and reported that they have lost Oliver to the police. Fagin is enraged.

More thieves show up: Bill Sikes and his dog; Nancy, Sikes's girlfriend; and Betsy. Fagin tells them that Oliver is a danger to them all because he may tell the police about them. Nancy poses as

Oliver's sister and goes to the police station to find out what happened and where Oliver is.

Brownlow asks Oliver to tell him his life's story, but this is interrupted by a visit from Mr. Grimwig, an argumentative old man who often says, "I'll eat my head." He says that he will eat his head if Oliver is anything other than a common thief, and Brownlow decides to test Oliver by giving him some books to return to the bookseller's, with money to pay his bill.

Oliver heads out on the errand but is intercepted by Nancy and Sikes, who take him back to Fagin's lair. Meanwhile, Brownlow and Grimwig have come to the unsettling conclusion that the boy has taken off with the books, the money, and the new clothes Brownlow gave him and that he really is a thief.

At Fagin's, Fagin threatens Oliver, but Nancy unexpectedly defends him, saying that if Fagin hurts him, she will personally hurt Fagin. Oliver is dressed in his old rags and locked up.

Back in Oliver's birth town, Mr. Bumble visits Mrs. Mann and tells her that he is going to London to appear in court in a settlement for two paupers. She tells him all is well at her house, except for Dick, who, she says, has been making trouble. The trouble is that he wants someone to help him write a letter to Oliver Twist before he dies. Bumble is horrified by this request and urges Mrs. Mann to lock Dick in the coal cellar.

In London, Bumble sees an advertisement

offering five guineas for any information about Oliver Twist. The ad was placed by Brownlow, and Bumble goes to his house and tells Brownlow about Oliver's poor origin and supposed bad behavior. This turns Brownlow against Oliver, and he forbids Mrs. Bedlow to mention him again.

At Fagin's, Oliver is told that if he continues to resist, he will be hanged for theft. Fagin keeps him locked up, and Bates and the Dodger try to convince him to become a thief. Fagin, who comes in with another thief named Tom Chitling, who has just gotten out of jail, agrees.

On a nasty night, Fagin creeps out and heads over to Sikes's place, where he tells Sikes that he has a plan for a burglary in Chertsey. Sikes says that it can't be done; another thief, Toby Crackit, has looked the place over and found that he can't entice any of the servants to come in on the plan. Sikes finally says that they can get into the house but only if they have a boy small enough to get through a tiny window and then unlock the door. Fagin likes this plan because, even if they get caught, Oliver's prospects for a normal life will be ruined and he will have to continue his life of crime.

Chapters Twenty through Thirty-One

Nancy shows up to take Oliver to Sikes's place and confesses to him that she wants to help him but can't do anything right now. She tells him it will be good for them both if he keeps quiet about her being on his side.

Media Adaptations

Oliver Twist was adapted as a silent film in 1909, directed by J. Stuart Blackton and starring William Humphrey and Elita Proctor Otis; in 1912, directed by Thomas Bentley; and in 1916, directed by James Young and starring Marie Doro and Tully Marshal.

- The book was adapted as a film in 1922, directed by Frank Lloyd and starring Jackie Coogan and Lon Chaney; in 1933, directed by William J. Cowen and starring Dicke Moore and Irving Pichel; and in 1948, directed by David Leon and starring John Howard Davies and Alec Guinness.

- Television versions were released in 1959, directed by Daniel Petrie and starring Richard Thomas and Eric Portman; in 1982, directed by Clive Donner and starring Richard Charles and George C. Scott; in 1985, directed by Gareth Davies and starring Ben Rodska and Eric Porter; in 1997, directed by Tony Bill and starring Alex Trench and Richard Dreyfuss; and in 1999 starring Sam Smith and Robert Lindsay, directed by Renny Rye.

- A long-running Broadway musical based on *Oliver Twist*, entitled *Oliver!*, was adapted as a feature film in 1968, directed by Carol Reed.

Sikes and Oliver set out on the long journey to the house the gang will rob. At a deserted old house, they meet Barney, who is occasionally a waiter in a seedy bar in Saffron Hill, and Toby Crackit, the well-known burglar. In the middle of the night, they head out. Oliver is petrified and doesn't want to participate in the crime, but Sikes tells him he will kill him if he doesn't. Sikes opens a tiny window and tells Oliver to enter and open the door for the rest of the gang. Oliver goes in, planning to wake up the people inside and warn them, but they have already heard the break-in, and they shoot at Oliver and the other burglars. Toby and Sikes run off, with

Oliver, who is bleeding.

Back in the workhouse, Mrs. Corney, the matron, is making tea. Mr. Bumble visits her and notices that she's doing very well from defrauding the poor; she has good food, silver teaspoons, and nice furniture. He decides it would be in his best interest to marry the widow, so he flirts with her.

They are interrupted by a pauper who says that another pauper, old Sally, is dying and wants to speak to Mrs. Corney. Sally tells Mrs. Corney that many years ago she nursed a poor unmarried woman who had a child and then died. Before she died, she gave something made of gold to Sally. Sally kept it instead of giving it to the child, who, if he had received it and had known something about his mother, could have been proud of his origins. Sally's last words are, "They called him Oliver.... The gold I stole was—" but she dies before she can finish the sentence.

Toby Crackit returns to Fagin's and tells Fagin that the burglary fell apart and they had to leave the wounded Oliver behind in a ditch. Fagin is enraged, even more so because Toby has no idea where Sikes is either.

Fagin goes to the Three Cripples, the public house where Barney works. The landlord says Barney hasn't been heard from either. Fagin asks for a man named Monks, and the landlord says Monks will show up soon.

Fagin goes to Sikes's, where Nancy is alone and upset. She says she would rather that Oliver be dead than that he return to Fagin's clutches. This angers Fagin, and he leaves. As he walks the dark streets, someone calls out to him. It's Monks. Fagin lets him into his house and they talk. Monks insists that Fagin could have made a thief out of the boy, and Fagin says he has done everything he could. They see a shadow and fear that a woman is eavesdropping on them, but they can't find anyone.

Back at Mrs. Corney's, Bumble proposes marriage to her, and she agrees, telling him that she will tell him the rest of Sally's story about the golden treasure after they're married.

At the scene of the robbery, Oliver wakes up in the ditch, injured and exhausted. He drags himself back to the house, where he is taken in and the servants gloat over capturing one of the burglars. The lady of the house, Mrs. Maylie, and her adopted niece Rose, are surprised to find that the dangerous burglar is only a small boy, and they feel sorry for him. The doctor, Mr. Losberne, agrees to question Oliver in the ladies' presence. The doctor also says he will get the servants, Giles and Brittles, who fired at Oliver, to cooperate. He then talks to them and confuses them about whether or not they can be sure Oliver was actually the boy who was involved in the robbery. This also confuses two London detectives, Blathers and Duff, and they return to London without arresting Oliver.

Chapters Thirty-Two through Forty-One

Oliver's broken arm heals under the care of Rose Maylie, Mrs. Maylie, and Mr. Losberne. They take a trip to London so that Oliver can see Mr. Brownlow, and Oliver points out the ruined house where the robber gang met. The doctor jumps out of the carriage and goes into the building, where he finds an ugly, deformed man who says he has lived alone there for twenty-five years.

At Brownlow's house, they find a "For Rent" sign in the window, and neighbors tell them Brownlow has gone to the West Indies with Mrs. Bedlow and Mr. Grimwig. Oliver is deeply disappointed because he knows that Brownlow must have decided that he really was a thief when he did not return when Brownlow sent him out on his errand to the bookseller's.

The group goes on to a rural cottage, where they spend the summer, and Oliver is healed and enchanted by the beautiful countryside.

During this peaceful time, Rose Maylie becomes ill with a dangerous fever. Mrs. Maylie writes to Mr. Losberne and to "Harry Maylie, Esquire." Oliver takes the letters to the nearest village to deliver them, and he runs into a tall man wearing a cloak, who swears at him and then falls down in a fit of convulsions.

Harry Maylie, who is Mrs. Maylie's son, arrives. He is deeply in love with Rose, but Mrs. Maylie tells him that Rose will probably refuse to marry him because there is some sort of scandal attached to her and that if she becomes his wife, she will ruin his future career.

One day soon after, Oliver has a nightmare about Fagin and wakes to see Fagin looking at him through the window. He tells the others, but they can't find any evidence that anyone has been outside the window.

Harry asks Rose to marry him, and, as predicted, she says that she does love him but can't marry him because it will attach scandal to his name. Disappointed, Harry leaves, but he makes Oliver promise to write him regularly and tell him what is happening in the Maylie household.

At the workhouse, Mr. Bumble and Mrs. Corney (now Mrs. Bumble) have been married for eight weeks. They fight constantly. Mr. Bumble is now subservient to her wicked temper and physical abuse. As a result, he goes to a public house to drown his sorrows. At the pub, he meets a mysterious man in a cloak, who asks Mr. Bumble for information about Oliver Twist's birth. Mr. Bumble tells the man that his wife has this information and will give it up for money. They arrange a meeting the next day at an address in a seedy part of town. The man's name, he says, is Monks.

At the meeting, Mrs. Bumble tells Monks that Sally stole a locket and a wedding ring from Oliver's mother. It is inscribed with the name "Agnes" and a date that is a year before Oliver's birth. He gives her a payment of twenty-five pounds, takes the ring and locket, and throws them into the river, where they will be lost forever.

At Sikes's house Sikes is ill and wretched, but Fagin, the Artful Dodger, and Charley Bates show up with food, drink, and a little money. They go back to Fagin's to get the money, and everyone except Nancy leaves. Monks shows up, and Nancy eavesdrops on their conversation. The reader is not told what she hears.

When Fagin returns and gives her the money for Sikes, Nancy leaves. She's very upset and distraught, and Sikes notices that she's behaving strangely. He decides she must have a fever. She puts a sleeping potion in his drink, and when he falls asleep, she leaves and goes to a hotel, where Rose Maylie is staying. She tells Rose that she is the one who grabbed Oliver to take him back to the thieves but that she regrets it. She then asks Rose if she knows Monks. Rose doesn't, but Nancy tells her, "He knows you." She tells Rose that she learned of her and found out where she was staying by eavesdropping on Monks and Fagin.

Monks, she says, offered to pay Fagin for finding Oliver and to pay him more if Fagin could turn him into a thief. She later heard him say that all evidence of Oliver's true identity is gone and that Monks has his money. Despite this, he wanted Oliver to suffer, to be imprisoned and worse, and he would devote his life to ruining Oliver's. Monks also said that Mrs. Maylie and Rose would give a fortune to know where Oliver is.

Rose offers to protect Nancy if she will turn

away from the thieves, but Nancy says it's too late. She tells Rose she will walk on London Bridge every Sunday night, in case Rose wants to talk to her again. Rose writes to Harry, asking him what to do about this situation.

Oliver enters, excited because he has seen Mr. Brownlow entering a house. Rose takes Oliver to the house, and they have a joyous reunion. Rose discusses Nancy's revelations with Mr. Brownlow, and Brownlow recruits Mr. Losberne and Harry Maylie.

Chapters Forty-Two through Fifty-One

On the same night that Rose and Nancy meet, Noah Claypole and Charlotte come to London. They have stolen a twenty-pound note, and, by chance, they stop at the Three Cripples, the thieves' pub. Fagin overhears them talking about their crime and the difficulty of cashing such a big note without arousing suspicion, and he offers to take them in and teach them. He tells them that one of his best thieves, the Artful Dodger, has been arrested and could end up a "lifer."

Charley Bates arrives and explains that there are witnesses to the crime, so the Dodger's fate is sealed. Shamefully enough, the stolen item was a small snuffbox, not even anything expensive or daring. Fagin tells him that Dawkins will perform well at the trial and will uphold his dignity as a daring thief. Claypole is sent to the police station to see how the hearing goes; the Dodger mocks everyone there.

The following Sunday night, Nancy tries to leave to go to London Bridge, in case the Maylies are there to meet her. Sikes senses something amiss and refuses to let her go. Fagin assumes she has another boyfriend and plots to convince her to turn against Sikes and perhaps poison him. This will be convenient for Fagin, who thinks Sikes knows too much. He decides to have her followed so he can find out where her real affections lie. Then he can use the information against her and convince her to do Sikes in. He assigns Claypole to this job.

A week later, Nancy goes to London Bridge, followed by Claypole. Brownlow tells Nancy that he wants to get the secret of Oliver's identity out of Monks and that he also wants her to turn Fagin over to him. She refuses to betray either of them but tells him that if he goes to the Three Cripples, he can see Monks there. She describes him, and it turns out that the description is familiar to Brownlow—it matches someone he already knows.

Fagin is furious that Nancy talked to Brownlow, and in his anger he recruits Sikes by telling him that Nancy did so and that Noah can prove it. Sikes runs home and locks Nancy in and then tells her everything she said was heard by Claypole. She begs him to spare her life, but he is unmoved and kills her.

He is horrified by what he's done and runs outside with his dog, wandering aimlessly, feeling pursued and haunted. He realizes that people may be on the hunt for a murderer with a dog, so he tries to drown the dog, but the dog escapes.

Meanwhile, Brownlow has abducted Monks from the Three Cripples and brought him to his house. Brownlow tells Monks he must cooperate or Brownlow will give him to the police and charge him with fraud and robbery.

It turns out that Monks's father and Brownlow were friends for many years. When Monks's father was a boy, his sister, who was going to marry Brownlow, died. Brownlow and Monks's father were always close after that.

Monks's father was forced by his parents to marry. They chose a woman ten years older, who was greedy and evil. They had one son, Monks. The couple eventually separated, and the woman went to Europe, taking the young Monks with her. Eventually, Monks's father met a new love, a girl of nineteen, and became engaged. Monks's father then inherited money from a relative in Rome, but while there, he contracted a fatal illness. When his ex-wife heard about this, she went to see him, and when he died, she and her son, Monks, inherited all the money.

Brownlow tells Monks that before Monks's father left England, he left a portrait of his new love with Brownlow. Brownlow was unable to find the girl or her family after Monks's father's death.

Brownlow tells Monks that he was startled by Oliver's resemblance to this portrait and that he knew Monks might know who Oliver was. Monks had gone to the West Indies, so Brownlow followed him there and then followed him back to London. Brownlow tells Monks that he knows Monks's father made a will that contained the secret of Oliver's identity but that Monks's mother destroyed it so that she and Monks could keep all the money.

Monks breaks down and says he will confess all the facts in front of witnesses and in writing. Brownlow says that he must also give back Oliver's share of the inheritance. Monks agrees.

Mr. Losberne enters and says that Sikes's dog has been found and a huge manhunt is on for him. Also, he says, Fagin will soon be arrested.

Meanwhile, Toby Crackit, Chitling, and Kags, a convict, have gathered in a decrepit old house on an island in the Thames. After dark, Sikes appears. They are horrified by him because, although they're thieves, they're not murderers, at least not of women. A crowd gathers outside, yelling that Sikes is inside. He tries to escape by shinning down a rope from the chimney of the house but slips into a loop he has made and inadvertently hangs himself.

Two days later, Mrs. Maylie, Rose, Mr. Losberne, and Mrs. Bedwin travel toward Oliver's birthplace. Behind them, Mr. Brownlow and Monks follow. In a meeting, Mr. Brownlow tells Monks, "This child is your half-brother; the illegitimate son of your father, my dear friend Edwin Leeford, by poor young Agnes Fleming, who died in giving him birth."

Monks agrees. Agnes Leeford was his father's young sweetheart, and he had planned to marry her, as shown by the ring he gave her and the locket with her name on it. He had written a will, which allotted an annual income of eight hundred pounds each to Monks and his mother and which gave the rest of the property to Agnes and her unborn child. If the child was a boy, he was to receive the money only if he had led a clean, honorable life. If he had not, his money was to go to Monks.

Monks says that his mother burned the will, and he swore to her that he would find the child, if it lived, and make its life a misery.

Mr. and Mrs. Bumble are then brought in and forced to confess that Mrs. Bumble stole the locket and ring that were once Agnes's.

Brownlow then says that Agnes had a much younger sister and that after her father died, she was adopted by some country people. Monks's mother tracked her down and told the new parents that she was illegitimate and thus tainted. This scandal marked her life, and she was treated poorly until Mrs. Maylie noticed her and took her away. Thus, Oliver is Rose's nephew. Also, Rose's previous reluctance to marry Harry, because of her belief that the scandal attached to her would taint him, is eliminated now that she has a respectable origin. They become engaged.

Chapters Fifty-Two and Fifty-Three

Fagin is in court, and the verdict is "Guilty." He is sentenced to death by hanging. He realizes that, of all the people in the courtroom, none care about him and all are glad he will die. Brownlow and Oliver visit him in his cell, and Brownlow asks about some papers that Monks gave to Fagin. Fagin tells him where the papers are. Oliver is so upset by this visit that he is unable to walk for some time afterward.

A few months later, Rose and Harry are married, and Harry gives up his plans for a political career in favor of life as a clergyman. Mrs. Maylie comes to live with them in their country parsonage. Oliver generously allows Monks to keep half of the inheritance, and Monks goes to the New World and eventually dies in prison. The rest of Fagin's gang are transported far from England and die overseas. Mr. Brownlow adopts Oliver as his son, and they live with Mrs. Bedwin, close to Rose and Harry's parsonage. Mr. Losberne and Mr. Grimwig also settle close by. Noah and Charlotte Claypole become police informers; they buy drinks on Sundays and then report on the pubs for being open, which is against the law on Sunday. The Bumbles lose their jobs and become so poverty-stricken that they must live in the workhouse they once ran. Charley Bates repents of his life of crime and becomes a wholesome farmer.

Characters

Artful Dodger

See Jack Dawkins

Barney

Barney is a waiter at the Three Cripples, a pub where the thieves hang out. He has a nasal condition, so everything he says sounds like he has a cold.

Charley Bates

Charley Bates is a member of Fagin's gang and is most notable for his habit of laughing all the time, even when it's inappropriate.

Mrs. Bedwin

Mrs. Bedwin is a comforting, motherly old woman, very clean and neat. She is Mr. Brownlow's housekeeper and takes care of Oliver when Mr. Brownlow takes him in. Even when Mr. Brownlow becomes disillusioned about Oliver's true nature, her faith in Oliver never wavers.

Betsy

Betsy is a member of Fagin's gang; she is not really pretty but is healthy looking and loyal to the gang.

The Bookseller

The bookseller runs the book stall where Mr. Brownlow stands reading when the Artful Dodger and Charley Bates pick his pockets. They run away, and Oliver is accused of the crime, but the bookseller follows him to court and insists on testifying that he is innocent. He is "an elderly man with decent but poor appearance."

Brittles

Brittles is a servant of Mrs. Maylie's. Although he is over thirty years old, he is considered a "boy" by the others in the household, indicating that he may be a little slow.

Mr. Brownlow

Mr. Brownlow is a wealthy, respectable gentleman, well educated, moderate, and kind. At first he believes that Oliver has stolen from him but soon realizes this is wrong and takes Oliver in and has his housekeeper, Mrs. Bedwin, nurse him back to health. When Oliver disappears again, he believes Oliver truly was a thief, but he is ready to renounce this view when Oliver comes back into his life. He does all he can to help Oliver and to restore him to his relatives and a respectable life. Dickens describes him as having "a heart large enough for any six ordinary old gentlemen of humane disposition."

Mr. Bumble

Mr. Bumble is the parish beadle, a position of petty and pompous authority that fills him with a sense of his own importance. He is a bully and loves to abuse people whom he knows can't fight back, but when he is faced with anyone stronger, he's a coward. He's also greedy: he marries Mrs. Corney simply because she seems rich and receives his just reward of a bitterly unhappy marriage.

Charlotte

Charlotte is the Sowerberrys's maid; she is strong but slovenly and lazy. She later joins Noah Claypole in a life of crime.

Tom Chitling

Tom Chitling is one of Fagin's gang. He is about eighteen, not very bright, and has small eyes and a pock-marked face.

Noah Claypole

Noah is a charity boy who works for Mr. Sowerberry and who abuses Oliver simply because he can: Oliver is smaller than Noah, and lower in the social order. Noah is big, clumsy, greedy, cowardly, and lazy. He later joins Fagin's gang, using the alias "Morris Bolter," and asks Fagin for easy, safe jobs; he first specializes in taking money from children sent on errands and later becomes an informer, telling the police about pubs that are illegally open on Sunday.

Mrs. Corney

Mrs. Corney oversees the workhouse where Oliver was born. She is a widow but later marries Mr. Bumble, whom she terrorizes with her temper and her physical and verbal abuse. She hates the paupers and considers them an annoyance; she doesn't even see them as human and has no sympathy for them even when they are dying of starvation and disease.

Toby Crackit

Toby Crackit is a well-known burglar who works with Fagin and Sikes; unlike them, he is flamboyant.

Jack Dawkins

Also called the Artful Dodger, Dawkins is the best thief in Fagin's gang. He wears a man's coat with the sleeves turned up and is street-smart beyond his years. He is eventually caught for pick-pocketing, but he swaggers and brags and is disrespectful to everyone in court.

Dick

Dick is Oliver's best friend at Mrs. Mann's "infant farm." The two of them have stuck together through their shared experiences of beatings, starvation, and neglect. Like Oliver, Dick has a pure soul and remains kind, sweet, and trusting until his early death from illness.

Fagin

Fagin is a master criminal, the head of a gang of child thieves, whom he trains and uses, taking half of their income. He is ugly and filthy, with red hair and a matted red beard, and he has no loyalty to anyone or anything but himself; he easily turns against Bill Sikes, for example, and tries to get Nancy, Sikes's girlfriend, to kill him. He is eventually caught and sentenced to death. He goes mad when he realizes that no one in the world cares about him and that the spectators are all happy that he will be hanged.

Mr. Fang

Mr. Fang is the magistrate who deals with Oliver when he is accused of stealing. He is notorious for his strictness and inflexibility, and he is completely uninterested in the facts of the matter, until a witness whose testimony can't be denied steps in and speaks in Oliver's favor.

Agnes Fleming

Agnes Fleming is the daughter of a retired naval officer. She appears at the workhouse to give birth to Oliver, but no one knows her name, where she came from, or who her relatives are until the end of the book. Her sister is Rose Maylie's mother, so Oliver and Rose are cousins.

Gamfield

Gamfield is a chimney sweep who sees an advertisement offering five pounds to anyone who will take Oliver off the parish's hands. He is eager to get the money and applies to be Oliver's master, but at the last minute he is refused when a kindly magistrate sees that Oliver is deeply afraid of him.

Mr. Giles

Mr. Giles is Mrs. Maylie's butler. When the gang of thieves puts Oliver through the window of Mrs. Maylie's house, Giles shoots at Oliver, unaware that he is just a boy. Even after he finds out, however, he enjoys the sense that he is a hero and doesn't tell those who are praising him that he has defended the house from a child. Despite his exalted sense of his own importance, he is basically good at heart, loyal, and agreeable.

Mr. Grimwig

Mr. Grimwig is a friend of Mr. Brownlow's.

He is a retired lawyer and has a habitually argumentative personality, perhaps as a remnant of his law days. He is heavy, old, lame in one leg, and he carries a heavy stick, which he likes to pound on the ground to make his point. His favorite expression is "I'll eat my head," which he says when he doesn't believe something is true.

Kags

Kags is a robber who was transported overseas as punishment for his crime—presumably to Australia, although Dickens doesn't make this clear. He has returned to London, and his past has marked his face: he is "a robber of fifty years, whose nose had been almost beaten in."

Edward Leeford

See Monks

Mr. Limbkins

Mr. Limbkins is the head of the parish board, which oversees the welfare of the poor. He is very fat and has a very red face; like many of the other functionaries in the book, he actually does little to help anyone other than himself.

Mr. Losberne

Mr. Losberne is a surgeon who is called when Oliver is found injured after the attempted burglary of Mrs. Maylie's house. He is good-humored and quick-witted, as is shown by the way he confuses Giles, Brittles, and the London detectives assigned to the burglary case. Like Mr. Brownlow, he believes in Oliver's essential goodness and is devoted to helping him.

Mrs. Mann

Mrs. Mann is a harsh old woman who runs a foster home; she takes in pauper children and raises them, and the parish gives her an allowance for the upkeep of each child. She pockets this money, starves the children, and otherwise abuses them. The corrupt system is revealed by the fact that whenever she is investigated after a child's death from starvation, illness, or neglect, the investigators blithely state that the death was "accidental" and continue sending children, and money, to her.

Harry Maylie

Harry is Mrs. Maylie's son. He is about twenty-five, good-looking, with an easy, pleasant demeanor. He is deeply in love with Rose and wants to marry her even if she has some scandal in her background.

Mrs. Maylie

Mrs. Maylie is Rose's adoptive aunt. She is a well-mannered, genteel, elderly woman. She is generous and loving, as shown by her adoption of

Rose and her equal kindness to Oliver.

Rose Maylie

Rose, like Oliver, is a sweet, generous, loyal, and optimistic person. She is Agnes Fleming's younger sister and Oliver's aunt, although she doesn't know this until the end of the book. For most of the book, she and the others believe there is some sort of scandal attached to her origins; for this reason, she refuses to marry Harry Maylie, although she deeply loves him, because she doesn't want his career marred by her low origins. Later, when her name is cleared, they enjoy a happy marriage.

Monks

Toward the end of the book, the reader learns that Monks's true name is Edward Leeford. He is Oliver's half-brother and has sworn to spend his life ruining Oliver's, because if he does so, he can keep the money he illegally inherited from their father. He has spent his life in crime, and even when Oliver splits the inheritance with him to allow him the resources to lead an honest life, he continues as a criminal and eventually dies overseas.

Nancy

Nancy, like Betsy, might have been pretty once, but her rough life has made her untidy and ill mannered. However, she still has some nobility of soul left, as shown by the fact that she regrets bringing Oliver back to the gang and later tries to help him get free of them, despite the fact that she knows the gang will kill her if they find out.

Bill Sikes

Bill Sikes is the most notorious and ruthless member of Fagin's gang; he is strong, impulsive, and dangerous. Dickens remarks that he has the sort of legs that "always look in an unfinished and incomplete state without a set of fetters to garnish them." He later murders Nancy, his girlfriend, when he hears that she has turned against the gang, and he is pursued throughout London until he accidentally hangs himself while trying to escape. Dickens accentuates his inhumane personality when he has Sikes try to kill his own dog, lest the dog lead pursuers to him.

Mr. Sowerberry

Mr. Sowerberry is a tall, gaunt, mournful-looking man, befitting his profession as undertaker. He takes on Oliver as an apprentice and teaches him the trade.

Mrs. Sowerberry

Meaner than her husband, Mrs. Sowerberry is short and thin, with a sharp face and a nasty disposition. She becomes jealous of Oliver when she sees that her husband favors him and so treats Oliver badly.

Sally Thingummy

Sally is a withered old pauper who serves as a midwife at Oliver's birth, despite the fact that she is somewhat drunk. She later dies in the workhouse, but not before she reveals some secrets about Oliver's mother.

Oliver Twist

Oliver is born in a workhouse to an unknown woman whose name, the reader learns much later, is Agnes Fleming. He is sensitive, compassionate, kind, loyal, and gentle, and no matter how much he is abused and mistreated, he retains these qualities as well as his deep faith in the innate goodness of people. At times he seems rather naïve; for example, when he sees the members of Fagin's gang practicing picking Fagin's pockets and when he goes out with them to steal but has no idea they are thieves until they run off and he is apprehended for the deed. An example of his loyalty is his love for his childhood friend Dick; when he goes back to the workhouse, his first thought is to find Dick, and he is crushed to learn that Dick has since died. Although he is badly treated by many people in the book and comes to fear them, he never hates them. Similarly, although Monks has spent most of his life trying to ruin Oliver's, Oliver has no hard feelings against him and divides his own inheritance with Monks, although Monks is legally entitled to nothing.

Good and Evil

According to George Gissing in *Critical Study of the Works of Charles Dickens*, Dickens once wrote, "I wished to show, in little Oliver, the principle of good surviving through every adverse circumstance, and triumphing at last." The novel does this but perhaps at the cost of depicting Oliver as a realistic character. Although he runs away from Mr. and Mrs. Sowerberry, in the remainder of the novel Oliver has little initiative or drive. He is the tool of thieves or the protégé of kind Samaritans, but he never purposefully seeks his own life or decides, on his own, what he must do.

Nevertheless, the pattern of good versus evil runs throughout the book; generally, the good people, like Oliver, Mr. Brownlow, and the Maylies, are very good, and the bad people, such as Fagin, Monks, and Sikes, are thoroughly bad.

A rare exception is Nancy, who has led a corrupt life but who nevertheless yearns to protect Oliver and do some good. Despite these desires, however, she is so sunk in her own miserable life that she doesn't believe she can ever change; she feels she is doomed to die at the hands of the criminals, and she turns out to be right.

Other characters, such as Mr. Bumble and Mr.

Fang, are presented as holders of positions of public trust who are nevertheless evil and untrustworthy. These characters, and the corrupt-but-good ones like Nancy, were intended to shock readers of Dickens's time out of their traditional class-based views, which held that the poor were often corrupt and criminal, whereas those who were wealthy or in high positions were automatically moral. One of the most corrupt and scheming people in the book is Monks's mother, a high-born and wealthy woman who proves to be an evil and selfish manipulator.

Satire of the Poor Laws

Throughout the book, Dickens shows, and comments on, the effects of the laws on the poor. Confined to workhouses, starved, and mistreated, the poor have no way of redeeming themselves from unending misery and death except by running away or turning criminal. Statistics show that crime soared after the Poor Laws of 1834, despite the government's exultation that much money would be saved on feeding, housing, and clothing them.

Dickens shows the effects of the Poor Laws in his depiction of the criminal underworld of London as well as through dark, mocking humor, as when Mr. Bumble and Mr. Sowerberry are discussing the low price the parish board will pay for coffins. When Sowerberry complains about the small prices, Mr. Bumble remarks with a laugh that the coffins are correspondingly small, so Sowerberry is not losing much. The coffins are small because they're made for children who died of neglect or starvation; the men's laughter only serves to show their callousness and the callousness of the public in allowing such things to happen. Dickens also mocks authority figures' fear of the poor, as when Oliver is locked up for the "crime" of asking for more food. In addition, he enlists the reader on his side by saying that unsympathetic people, who are not upset by the fact that Oliver had to eat food even the dog wouldn't touch, should be as hungry as Oliver was and have to eat such food themselves.

Alienation

Many, if not most, of the characters in the book are alienated from their society and each other. Oliver is an orphan, the quintessential outcast, and with the exception of Dick, the people with whom he associates throughout his childhood are deeply selfish and mistrustful, interested in their own welfare and no one else's. Among the thieves, there is no camaraderie; they often spy on each other and are ready to turn on each other at a moment's notice if it will gain them more money or freedom from jail. The "good" characters in the book present a rare little community of trust and goodwill, but they are so good that at times they seem unrealistic: no quarrel or misunderstanding ever mars their pleasant society. In addition, they are a small minority compared to the vast number of other characters in the book, most of whom are solitary and cut off from their origins and families, or associate in rough, shifting, untrustworthy, and temporary alliances.

Shifting Narrative Voice

Throughout the novel, Dickens employs a shifting narrative voice; as James R. Kincaid noted in *Dickens and the Rhetoric of Laughter*, "It is impossible to define the characteristics or moral position of the narrators in this novel, for they are continually shifting." At times the narrator is detached and wordy, as in the opening paragraph in which he says abstractly that he will not name the town or workhouse where a certain "item of mortality" was born. At the same time, he is mocking the conventions of many novels of his time, which open with a lengthy and often smug description of the main character's birthplace and family.

The narrator doesn't consistently stay in this remote but sarcastic voice but sometimes shifts to remarking ironically on the supposedly wonderful way in which the poor are treated and on how kind it is; or sometimes the narrator appeals to the friendly feeling of the reader: "We all know how chilled and desolate the best of us will sometimes feel." As Kincaid noted, "We can never count on being in any single relationship with the narrative voice for long. Just as we relax…. We are pushed away."

Topics for Further Study

- Oliver Twist attacks the nineteenth-century treatment of orphans by showing how they were abused. How are orphans treated in our society? Investigate and write about what happens to children whose parents are dead or unknown, and who don't have family members willing to take them.

- Fagin is sentenced to death for his crimes. Do you think this is justified? Why or why not?

- Oliver is remarkably "good," despite the starvation and abuse he receives during his childhood. Do you think this is realistic? Why or why not?

- Investigate what it was like to live in London during the middle of the nineteenth century. If you lived there, what job would you have done? What would your life have been like?

- Fagin is evil and cunning, and Dickens also frequently mentions that he is Jewish, leading critics to remark that Dickens was anti-Semitic, though this may not have been the case. How common was anti-Semitism in Dickens's time? Research and write about how Jewish people were viewed and treated in England during the nineteenth century.

Dark Humor

The novel is filled with dark humor, from Mr. Bumble and Mr. Sowerberry laughing about the abundance of small children's coffins to Dickens's mocking the seriousness and puffery of the members of the parish board, to his exposure of the cowardice and avarice of Noah and Charlotte, to the caperings of the Artful Dodger when he is put on trial. This humor only serves to sharpen the desperate sufferings of Oliver and the other characters, however, so that although readers may laugh while they are reading the book, when they're done, they tend to remember the sadness in it.

Characterization

Dickens uses "flat" characters; his people don't tend to grow or change over the course of the book. Oliver, who begins good, stays good, and he never wises up; never once does he show any awareness that the thieves are truly evil or any real disgust at Fagin's life. He is afraid of the thieves, but he is afraid because they may hurt him, not because he is aware that they're twisted and corrupted souls. Fagin, who begins evil, stays that way. Many of the characters are easily marked by certain "tags" of behavior or voice: Mr. Grimwig habitually thumps his cane on the ground and asserts, "I'll eat my head!"; Fagin is always out for money; Mr. Brownlow is steadfastly good; Monks is obsessively evil. Mr. Bumble is consistently pompous and shallow, and Noah Claypole remains a coward and a bully throughout the book.

In modern fiction, characters like these are considered a mark of poor writing, but in Dickens's time, readers were not bothered by such flat depictions. In addition, because the novel was written as a serial that required readers to remember all the characters for a long period of time, it was necessary for writers to make their characters easy to remember and categorize.

Historical Context

In the mid-nineteenth century, England was suffering from economic instability and widespread unemployment. The economic instability was a legacy of the Napoleonic era, which lasted until 1815. During this time, England was at war with France. The English government had imposed heavy taxes to pay for the war, and although these did not really affect the wealthy classes, they were a crushing burden on the poor. Prices rose, food became scarce, and inflation rose. Also because of the war, French and European markets for English goods were closed, leading to unemployment among workers.

Workers were also unemployed because the increasing use of machinery in manufacturing had made many of their jobs obsolete; for example, instead of employing many individual weavers, textile manufacturers began using mechanized looms, with only a few people needed to run them. The angry workers, known as Luddites, led movements to smash industrial machinery, a crime that was made punishable by death in 1811.

The Napoleonic War ended in 1815, but the misery did not. With the war over, England entered the worst depression it had ever seen. The number of poor people, never low, increased to crisis levels. Historically, each parish had been responsible for taking care of its poor by handing out money and food, and more and more people now chose to take these handouts. Others worked but took the assistance anyway, and when employers found out about this, they lowered their wages, making it impossible even for honest workers to survive on their wages. In addition, several thousand war veterans had returned to England, swelling the ranks of the jobless.

During this time, children often worked long hours, every day of the week, in dangerous factories. In 1833, child labor and working conditions began to be regulated and controlled.

In 1834, the "Poor Laws" were passed. They required that people needing public assistance live in workhouses, where they were poorly fed and badly treated. The object of this plan was to make public assistance unattractive to the poor and thus to decrease the number of people on assistance, as well as the associated costs. The plan did save money, but at a great cost in human suffering, as Dickens makes plain in *Oliver Twist*.

In 1837, Queen Victoria ascended the English throne and began her long rule and a relatively stable period in English history. This stability, and the increasing numbers of people in the middle classes who were educated enough to read books for leisure and had the money to buy them and the time to read them, would help the young Dickens to an illustrious future.

Critical Overview

In *Dickens and His Readers: Aspects of Novel Criticism Since 1836*, George H. Ford quoted George Borrow, who wrote in 1838 that "Everybody was in raptures over a certain *Oliver Twist* that had just come out." Readers of the time, far from being dismayed by the dark quality of the book, loved it. An exception was Thackeray, who mocked Dickens's portrayal of Nancy, saying she was sentimentally and unrealistically presented. Dickens was so upset by this comment that he wrote an angry reply to Thackeray in the preface to the book, according to Ford. Ford also noted that although most readers loved the book, some were indeed alienated: "the kind of reader who cannot bear to be ruffled by violent emotions."

Some of these readers were critics who were dismayed by its presentation of criminals, workhouse inmates, and illegitimacy. According to Ford, Henry Fox wrote that the book was "painful and revolting"; Fox quoted Lady Carlyle, who commented, "I know that there are such unfortunate beings as pick-pockets and street walkers … but I own I do not wish to hear what they say to one another." Fox also wrote that although the book seemed to be such a fad that few dared to speak against it, "I suspect, when the novelty and the fashion of admiring [it and other books] wear off, they will sink to their proper level."

For these readers, Dickens's attacks on the social institutions responsible for crime and poverty were not considered enough to make up for the fact that he was presenting indecent, wretched characters to his supposedly sheltered readers. However, in *Critical Studies of the Works of Charles Dickens*, George Gissing noted that these views were not shared by most readers and wrote, "When criticism had said its say, the world did homage to a genial moralist, a keen satirist, and a leader in literature."

Gissing did remark on what he saw as the book's flaws: "Attempting a continued story, the author shows at once his weakest side, the defect which he will never outgrow. There is no coherency in the structure of the thing; the plotting is utterly without ingenuity; the mysteries are so artificial as to be altogether uninteresting." However, he did note that at the time Dickens wrote the book, fiction was in its infancy, and readers were not nearly as demanding as they are now. Tight, complex, and realistic plotting had yet to be developed, so modern readers cannot fault Dickens for not using it. If modern readers overlook the creaky plot mechanisms, what remains is "a very impressive picture of the wretched and the horrible," with realistic descriptions of the London streets and people, their daily habits, voices, food, and clothing.

Compare & Contrast

- **1838:** It is not yet known that every person in the world has different fingerprints, so the criminal justice system relies on eyewitness reports, confessions, and rough clues to determine who has committed crimes.

Today: Fingerprinting, DNA analysis, and sophisticated analysis of microscopic clues left at crime scenes have made the criminal justice system much more precise than it was in Dickens's day.

- **1838:** Throughout the 1800s, a variety of crimes in England are punishable by death. In 1800, 200 types of crimes merited the death penalty. By 1837, reforms have diminished this number to 15 types of crimes.

  Today: In England, there is no death penalty for any crime.

- **1838:** Laws control the movement and daily lives of poor people who are confined to "workhouses" or "debtor's prisons" where they are starved and mistreated.

  Today: England has an extensive social welfare system, which provides aid to unemployed, ill, and elderly people.

Joseph Gold, in *Charles Dickens: Radical*

Moralist, wrote that it was not surprising that critics in Dickens's day were upset by the book, because what Dickens did was to "humanize the criminal. This was not readily forgiven, for to humanize the criminal is to show his relationship to the reader, who would prefer to regard him as another species." This was very different from previous novels, which either romanticized criminals as gallant outcasts or as complete monsters, utterly inhuman.

In *Modern Critical Views: Dickens*, J. Hillis Miller commented that the book was flawed mainly because of its depiction of Oliver, who from beginning to end is a tool of others. He does rebel against the thieves who try to mold him into one of them, but in the end he succumbs to the molding of Mr. Brownlow and friends; Mr. Brownlow adopts him, and he becomes what Brownlow wants him to be. He has not solved the dilemmas of his parentage and of determining on his own what he wants to be and to do. He lives happily ever after, but "only by living in a perpetual childhood of submission to protection and direction from without."

Geoffrey Thurley, in *The Dickens Myth*, remarked that of course the book's plot is absurd but that the book's enduring value stems from its "moral vision" and its depiction of the confrontation between good and evil.

In *Dickens: A Collection of Critical Essays*, John Bayley wrote that the book, unlike its predecessor, *The Pickwick Papers*, was "a modern novel," as shown by the fact that despite its flaws it can still touch the modern reader.

What Do I Read Next?

- Dickens's *The Pickwick Papers* (1836-1837) is a humorous satire on pre-Victorian London.

- Dickens's *David Copperfield* (1849-1850), drawn from Dickens's own early experiences, tells the story of a young orphan.

- *Bleak House*, by Dickens (1852-1853), is a satirical tale set in the labyrinth of the English legal system.

- Dickens's *A Tale of Two Cities* (1859) is a dramatic narrative of the French Revolution.

- Charlotte Brönte's *Jane Eyre* (1847) tells another story about an orphan in nineteenth-century England.

Sources

Bayley, John, "Things As They Really Are," in *Dickens: A Collection of Critical Essays*, edited by Martin Price, Prentice-Hall, 1967, pp. 83-96.

Ford, George H., *Dickens and His Readers: Aspects of Novel Criticism since 1836*, W. W. Norton and Company, 1965, pp. 35-47.

Gissing, George, *Critical Studies of the Works of Charles Dickens*, Haskell House, 1965, pp. 43-57.

Gold, Joseph, *Charles Dickens: Radical Moralist*, University of Minnesota Press, 1972, pp. 25-65.

Kincaid, James R., *Dickens and the Rhetoric of Laughter*, Oxford University Press, 1971, pp. 50-75.

Miller, J. Hillis, "The Dark World of Oliver Twist," in *Charles Dickens*, edited by Harold Bloom, Modern Critical Views series, Chelsea House, 1987, pp. 29-69.

Thurley, Geoffrey, *The Dickens Myth: Its Genesis and Structure*, St. Martin's Press, 1976, pp. 43-50.

For Further Reading

Fido, Martin, *The World of Charles Dickens: The Life, Times and Work of the Great Victorian Novelist*, Carlton, 1999.

> This book provides background information on Dickens's time, life, and work.

Hobsbaum, Philip, *A Reader's Guide to Charles Dickens*, Farrar, Straus and Giroux, 1972.

> This work examines all of Dickens's work and provides a guide to readers.

Kaplan, Fred, *Dickens: A Biography*, Johns Hopkins University Press, 1998.

> This biography of Dickens is written for high school students.

Pool, Daniel, *What Jane Austen Ate and Charles Dickens Knew: From Fox Hunting to Whist—The Facts of Daily Life in Nineteenth-Century England*, Touchstone Books, 1994.

> This fascinating volume explains all the customs of daily life in Dickens's time.